Bountiful Blessings

A Creative Devotional Experience

Susie Larson

Art by **Carolyn Williams**

BETHANYHOUSE

a division of Baker Publishing Group
Minneapolis, Minnesota

© 2018 by Susie Larson

Published by Bethany House Publishers
11400 Hampshire Avenue South
Bloomington, Minnesota 55438
www.bethanyhouse.com

Bethany House Publishers is a division of
Baker Publishing Group, Grand Rapids, Michigan

Printed in the United States of America

ISBN 978-0-7642-3023-3

Cover design by Dan Pitts

Author is represented by The Steve Laube Agency

18   19   20   21   22   23   24   7   6   5   4   3   2   1

To You, My Friend

God loves you with an everlasting love. He is faithful, wise, and true. He is a miracle-working, soul-saving, life-transforming God. And He cares deeply about you.

As you work your way through these pages, may you grow to know—on a much deeper level—what you possess when you have Christ. He is above all, in all, and through all. He is the way, the truth, and the life. He promises never to leave you, never to forsake you, and never to let go of your hand. Life on earth is hard sometimes, but life with God, even in the fiercest of storms, is always redemptive—and forever eternal. The Lord wants you to last long and finish strong, and He's the one who will keep you strong to the end.

May these blessings be yours in every way.

—Susie Larson

Blessed
in Every Way

And Jabez called on the God of Israel saying, "Oh, that You would bless me indeed, and enlarge my territory, that Your hand would be with me, and that You would keep me from evil, that I may not cause pain!" So God granted him what he requested.

1 Chronicles 4:10 (NKJV)

May the Lord enlarge your territory, expand your influence, and increase your capacity to walk in faith. May His hand of power be upon you in a way that marks everything you do. May He keep you from harm—both causing and enduring it—and may He use you to bless a world very much in need. And may He surprise you with breakthroughs and still-water Sabbath moments. Your Shepherd has placed His hand of blessing upon your head, and He will faithfully lead you. Have a lighthearted, joy-filled day today!

Look Up and Sing

What then shall we say to these things? If God is for us, who can be against us?

Romans 8:31 (NKJV)

When you are tempted to look down in despair, may you instead look up and declare, "My God is for me, who can stand against me?" When you are tempted to whine and grumble, may you instead dance and sing. When you are tempted to gossip or be petty, may you instead pray and intercede. God wants to bless the world through you! Look up today and rejoice. All of heaven is on your side.

Trust Him, He's Got You

The Lord himself goes before you and will be with you; he will never leave you nor forsake you. Do not be afraid; do not be discouraged.

Deuteronomy 31:8 (NIV)

May you rise up today with the full assurance that God has your back. He is with you, for you, and actively working on your behalf. He does for you what you cannot do for yourself. May you do for Him the one thing you can do: trust Him with your whole heart and embrace joy along the way. Grace and peace to you this day!

Embrace
Today's Grace

Not that I have already attained, or am already per-
fected; but I press on, that I may lay hold of that for
which Christ Jesus has also laid hold of me. Brethren,
I do not count myself to have apprehended; but one
thing I do, forgetting those things which are behind
and reaching forward to those things which are ahead,
I press toward the goal for the prize of the upward call
of God in Christ Jesus.

Philippians 3:12–14 (NKJV)

May you refuse to drag the heavy baggage from your past another step. May you refuse to borrow to-morrow's trouble when it's not yours to carry. May you instead grab hold of today's mercy, today's grace, and today's power offered you right here, right now, for this moment. May you walk in the delegated influence God has assigned you. Walk in a manner worthy of His name. And may holy confidence and humble dependence mark your life in every way today!

Fresh Favor
and Perspective

And the Lord will guide you continually and satisfy your desire in scorched places and make your bones strong; and you shall be like a watered garden, like a spring of water, whose waters do not fail.

Isaiah 58:11 (ESV)

May God Himself release fresh faith and perspective into your soul today! May He strengthen your frame and establish your steps. May He surround you with good friends who fear God and who love you. May He give you fresh vision for your future and divine wisdom for stewarding your "now" moments. May the song in your heart ring louder than the enemy's threats and accusations. There is no one like our God, and there is nothing like His love for you! Walk blessed today, because you are!

A Glimpse of Glory

He who believes in Me, as the Scripture has said, out
of his heart will flow rivers of living water.

John 7:38 (NKJV)

May God part the heavens and give you a glimpse
of how He sees you. May He open up your eyes
so you can see how much He loves you. May He awaken
your soul so you'll know healing and assurance like you've
never known before. And may His love pour in and through
you like a stream of living water. You're connected to the
supernatural Source of power—the Most High God. May
your understanding of what you possess in Him increase
exponentially today!

Healed, Strong, and Whole

Dear friend, I hope all is well with you and that you are
as healthy in body as you are strong in spirit.

3 John 1:2 (NLT)

May Jesus Himself lift you up and make you strong.
May He heal those hidden areas that surface time
and time again. May He bring wholeness and health to your
mind, body, and spirit. May He strengthen you and fill you
with faith so you'll dare to take the risks He puts before you.
May you take time in His presence so you'll remember how
strong and mighty He is. And may your day be filled with
sacred moments that remind you just how precious you are
to Him. You are so dear to His heart.

Springtime Expectancy

Be anxious for nothing, but in everything by prayer
and supplication, with thanksgiving, let your requests
be made known to God; and the peace of God, which
surpasses all understanding, will guard your hearts
and minds through Christ Jesus.

Philippians 4:6–7 (NKJV)

May God Himself put springtime in your soul. May
you live today with expectancy that He's doing a
new thing in your midst! May you refuse worry, release your
cares, and remember His promises. He'll make a way where
there seems to be no way. Have a faith-filled, expectant day
today!

Choose Life

I place before you Life and Death, Blessing and Curse.
Choose life so that you and your children will live. And
love God, your God, listening obediently to him, firmly
embracing him. Oh yes, he is life itself, a long life settled
on the soil that God, your God, promised to give your
ancestors, Abraham, Isaac, and Jacob.

Deuteronomy 30:19–20 (MESSAGE)

When the enemy tries to bait you into discouragement, may you instead take your courageous
stand in Christ Jesus. When the devil tries to seduce you into
despair, may you instead walk through the door of hope God
has provided for you. When you're tempted to walk down
jealousy's path, may you instead embrace your own beautiful purpose and take the high road God has set before you.
There's a best place for your feet today. Choose life today!

Joy and Strength

Consider it pure joy, my brothers and sisters, whenever you face trials of many kinds, because you know that the testing of your faith produces perseverance. Let perseverance finish its work so that you may be mature and complete, not lacking anything.

James 1:2–4 (NIV)

May God Himself fill you with pure joy amidst your trials. May you understand that He's developing perseverance in you so you'll be mature and complete, lacking in nothing. May you see the blessing in your battles. Instead of becoming self-conscious and wondering why so many arrows are aimed at you, may you simply become a better warrior. May you lay hold of the generous amounts of wisdom God has offered you in this place so that when it's all said and done, you're still standing. Have a great and victorious day.

Remember and Dream with God

For I know the plans I have for you, declares the Lord, plans for welfare and not for evil, to give you a future and a hope. Then you will call upon me and come and pray to me, and I will hear you. You will seek me and find me, when you seek me with all your heart.

Jeremiah 29:11–13 (ESV)

May you pause today, look back over your shoulder, and remember the ways God has been good to you, has come through for you, and has kept His word to you. May you look ahead in faith with expectancy, as you get a sense of the land He wants you to claim. May faith rise up within you as you take your first steps in that direction. And may you embrace a renewed resolve to walk intimately with the One who loves you and has a beautiful plan for your life. He deserves some sacred space in your day today! Blessings to you.

Fresh, Unfailing Mercies

Nothing, you see, is impossible with God.

Luke 1:37 (MESSAGE)

May God Himself wrap you up in His new mercies this day! Where you've known angst, may He give you awe-inspiring wonder. Where you've known heartbreak, may He bring healing, deliverance, and a supernatural breakthrough. May He help you blow the dust off your dreams and lift them up as possibilities once again. With God all things are possible. May you learn to pray from that beautiful truth. Be lifted up today. He's got you!

Worship Wins the Day

Oh come, let us sing to the Lord; let us make a joyful
noise to the rock of our salvation! Let us come into his
presence with thanksgiving; let us make a joyful noise
to him with songs of praise!

Psalm 95:1–2 (ESV)

May you awaken to the divine power of a grateful
heart. May you know there's victory in praise and
breakthrough in thanksgiving! When you stomp your feet,
raise your hands, and sing a song of praise, the enemy scur-
ries away and covers his ears, and his plans come to nothing.
With God on your side, you have all you need to win your
battles and grow in love. Sing a song of praise today even
while you wait for your breakthrough! A blessed day to you.

Filled to Overflowing

I pray that you, being rooted and established in love,
may have power, together with all the Lord's holy
people, to grasp how wide and long and high and
deep is the love of Christ, and to know this love that
surpasses knowledge—that you may be filled to the
measure of all the fullness of God.

Ephesians 3:17–19 (NIV)

May you experience increase in every way. May your capacity to know the heights of God's love grow exponentially. May your understanding of the depths of His faithfulness grow continually. May your belief in your divine value deepen tremendously. And, in the days ahead, may your willingness to trust God with every detail of your life change profoundly. You are deeply loved, deeply called, and profoundly cared for. May you live out this truth! Walk in humble confidence today.

Release Your Cares

We do not look at the things which are seen, but at the things which are not seen. For the things which are seen are temporary, but the things which are not seen are eternal.

2 Corinthians 4:18 (NKJV)

May God Himself surround you with His tender mercies and grace today. May He heal your soul so you can live by faith. Where you once reacted out of your insecurities, may you respond in faith, knowing you possess all in Christ. Where you once had a white-knuckled hold on your worries, may you release every care to Him and lift your hands in praise. You are not made for this world. You are only passing through. Live as the divinely loved and divinely called soul you are!

Simplify
and Refresh

May the God of hope fill you with all joy and peace in believing, so that by the power of the Holy Spirit you may abound in hope.

Romans 15:13 (ESV)

May God inspire you to tackle a project you've been putting off. May He motivate you to clean out the clutter and simplify your surroundings. May He refresh your weary soul and renew your tired mind. And in every way, may your soul be restored, your mind be renewed, and your spirit be at peace. He leads you by still waters; follow Him there. Be revived and refreshed this day!

Humility and Tenacity

Blessed are the meek, for they shall inherit the earth.

Matthew 5:5 (NKJV)

May God fill you with strength and power to embrace His grace this very hour. May you humble yourself before Him so that He may lift you up and bless you before a watching world. May you embrace a humble, teachable heart while maintaining tenacious and ferocious faith. May you bow low when He speaks and rise up when He tells you to move. Our God is King, and He moves mightily in and through His people. Live expectantly today!

Peace to Your Storm

Then He arose and rebuked the wind, and said to the sea, "Peace, be still!" And the wind ceased and there was a great calm.

Mark 4:39 (NKJV)

May Jesus speak peace to your soul and calm to your storm. May you sense His nearness even when the winds blow. May you know His joy and strength from the top of your head to the tips of your toes. May the hope He stirs in your heart cause you to live with a holy expectancy and trust that this storm too shall pass. And in the days ahead, may His very real love for you compel you to dance in the rain before the sun breaks through. He goes before you, He's got your back, and He's there, just around the bend. He'll never forsake you. Trust Him today!

Seated with Christ

Every valley shall be lifted up, and every mountain
and hill be made low; the uneven ground shall become
level, and the rough places a plain. And the glory of the
Lord shall be revealed, and all flesh shall see it together,
for the mouth of the Lord has spoken.

Isaiah 40:4–5 (ESV)

No matter if you're in the valley or on a mountain, may you remember that as a Christ-follower you are seated with Christ in the heavenly realms. Everything He has is yours. He has written your name on His hand and holds your desires close to His heart. Though the elements rage on earth, your footing is secure in Him. Stay hidden in the shelter of His wing; stay in that place of peace. May you remember today that nothing can separate you from His powerful, personal love for you. You're everything to Him.

Sowing and Reaping

Remember this: Whoever sows sparingly will also reap sparingly, and whoever sows generously will also reap generously. Each of you should give what you have decided in your heart to give, not reluctantly or under compulsion, for God loves a cheerful giver.

2 Corinthians 9:6–7 (NIV)

May God give you faith to sow seeds. May you become a purposeful, generous, faith-filled sower. May He supply and increase your store of seed and enlarge the harvest of your righteousness. May you be made rich in every way, generous in every occasion, and leave the world thanking God for your faithful soul! Rest well tonight, knowing your Father in heaven possesses all.

Fresh Joy, Fresh Faith

May you experience the love of Christ, though it is too great to understand fully. Then you will be made complete with all the fullness of life and power that comes from God.

Ephesians 3:19 (NLT)

May the God who created you fill you till you spill over with fresh joy and perspective. May the wisdom He imparts to you bless many as you speak life to those around you. May He stir up fresh, fiery faith to take on the mountains and put them under your feet. Overwhelming victory is yours because *you* are *His*.

Christ in Focus

We destroy arguments and every lofty opinion raised against the knowledge of God, and take every thought captive to obey Christ.

2 Corinthians 10:5 (ESV)

May God help you renew your mind and redeem your words. May you refuse thoughts that weaken you, thoughts that take your eyes off God. May you instead embrace thoughts that are true based on God's great love for you. May you refuse to speak about your life apart from faith. May you instead embrace faith, speak life, and choose life every single moment of every single day. Rest well.

The Battle Is the Lord's

The Lord will fight for you; you need only to be still.

Exodus 14:14 (NIV)

As you lie down to sleep, may the Lord Himself rise up and fight for you! May He draw by His Spirit your loved ones who do not love Him. May He bring the breakthrough where there's only been a roadblock. May you remember this day and every day that the battle is the Lord's! Rest, knowing God fights for you!

Abounding Grace

Each time [the Lord] said, "My grace is all you need.
My power works best in weakness." So now I am glad
to boast about my weaknesses, so that the power of
Christ can work through me.

2 Corinthians 12:9 (NLT)

May you—in spite of your mistakes and missteps—
see how God's love and provision more than cover
you. May you—in your weakness—experience abounding
grace that makes you divinely strong. Where you've experi-
enced loss and brokenness, may you know healing, wholeness, and redemption. Your Redeemer is for you and He is
faithful.

Gritty Faith

If God is for us, who can be against us? He who did not spare his own Son, but gave him up for us all—how will he not also, along with him, graciously give us all things? . . . No, in all these things we are more than conquerors through him who loved us.

Romans 8:31–32, 37 (NIV)

May the Lord Himself establish you in His best purposes for you. May He strengthen you with holy conviction and gritty faith to climb every mountain He's assigned to you. May He increase your capacity to love and encourage others. And when the enemy rises up against you, may you see with your own eyes how God fights for you. You're on the winning side. You can rest.

Equipped for Victory

"No weapon that is fashioned against you shall succeed, and you shall refute every tongue that rises against you in judgment. This is the heritage of the servants of the Lord and their vindication from me," declares the Lord.

Isaiah 54:17 (ESV)

Speak this over yourself: I am loved, called, and chosen. I am rich in every way and generous on every occasion. I'm anointed, appointed, equipped, and enabled by the power of God that works mightily within me! No weapon formed against me will prosper and no enemy scheme against me will succeed. I live, breathe, and serve powerfully under the shelter of the Most High God. Amen.

He Is Faithful

I wait quietly before God, for my victory comes from him. He alone is my rock and my salvation, my fortress where I will never be shaken.

Psalm 62:1–2 (NLT)

May God open the heavens, break through the clouds, and deliver the answer you've been waiting for. May He shore up your faith, strengthen your heart, and overwhelm you with His grace. May your soul know a peaceful assurance like it's never known before. May you believe from deep within that God is with you, God is for you, and He will never let you go. He is mighty to save.

The Rock

As for God, his way is perfect: The Lord's word is
flawless; he shields all who take refuge in him. For
who is God besides the Lord? And who is the Rock
except our God? It is God who arms me with strength
and keeps my way secure. He makes my feet like the
feet of a deer; he causes me to stand on the heights.

2 Samuel 22:31–34 (NIV)

May God's love and truth bring clarity and purpose
to your life. May His strength steady your steps.
May His compassion open your eyes and may His conviction make your heart beat strong. May His kingdom come
and His will be done in and through you. Rest in His truth.

Grateful Living

May the God of your father help you; may the Almighty bless you with the blessings of the heavens above, and blessings of the watery depths below, and blessings of the breasts and womb. May my fatherly blessings on you surpass the blessings of my ancestors, reaching to the heights of the eternal hills. May these blessings rest on the head of Joseph, who is a prince among his brothers.

Genesis 49:25–26 (NLT)

May you wrap your arms around the ones you love, look them in the eyes, and tell them how much you treasure them. May you look around and take notice of all the blessings you'd miss if they went away tomorrow. When you're tempted to indulge in melancholy or discontentment, may you instead jump up, raise your hands, and thank God for His daily and divine intervention in your life. May your humble gratitude give you keen spiritual insight and restful peace.

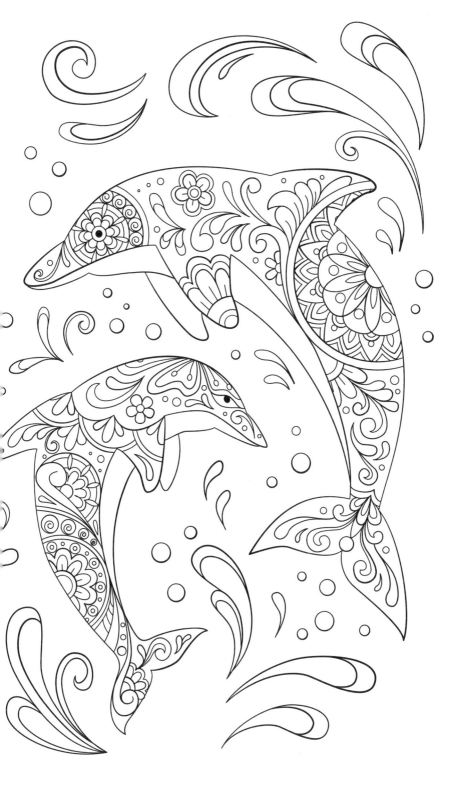

Freedom in Christ

For freedom Christ has set us free; stand firm therefore,
and do not submit again to a yoke of slavery.

Galatians 5:1 (ESV)

I t is *for* freedom that Christ has set you free. May you refuse to be subject to any yoke of slavery—slavery to sin, fear, legalism, or striving. May you rest in the knowledge that Jesus paid it all so that you could walk free and whole. May you boldly live the abundant, fruitful life He had in mind from the beginning. You are everything to Him.

Your New Future

The Lord says, "I will give you back what you lost to the swarming locusts, the hopping locusts, the stripping locusts, and the cutting locusts. It was I who sent this great destroying army against you. Once again you will have all the food you want, and you will praise the Lord your God, who does these miracles for you. Never again will my people be disgraced."

Joel 2:25–26 (NLT)

May God lift you up and heal and restore you fully. May you see glimpses of His glory everywhere you turn. May He show you wonders of His love that overwhelm you and make your knees weak. May He put a new song in your heart and a new dream in your spirit. May you walk forward unafraid and full of faith that your future will be far greater than your past.

Tomorrow's Promise

Don't be afraid—you're not going to be embarrassed.
Don't hold back—you're not going to come up short.
You'll forget all about the humiliations of your youth,
and the indignities of being a widow will fade from
memory. For your Maker is your bridegroom, his
name, God-of-the-Angel-Armies! Your Redeemer is
The Holy of Israel, known as God of the whole earth.

Isaiah 54:4–5 (MESSAGE)

May God expand your territory, enlarge your vision,
and increase your capacity for His influence in
your life. May you be quick to hear, quick to obey, and quick
to trust Him with every detail of your life. As you consider
His faithfulness today, may you walk faithfully to your next
place of promise tomorrow. He has been faithful. He *will* be
faithful. Rest assured that He's got you.

Secure in Christ

Through followers of Jesus like yourselves gathered in churches, this extraordinary plan of God is becoming known and talked about even among the angels! All this is proceeding along lines planned all along by God and then executed in Christ Jesus. When we trust in him, we're free to say whatever needs to be said, bold to go wherever we need to go.

Ephesians 3:10–12 (MESSAGE)

May you understand on a greater level your secure standing in Christ. May you approach Him with fresh boldness and faith, assured of His glad welcome. May your prayers move heaven and earth, and may you remember that everywhere you place your feet, God's kingdom comes to earth.

Your Story and God's

Always be full of joy in the Lord. I say it again—rejoice!
Let everyone see that you are considerate in all you do.
Remember, the Lord is coming soon.

Philippians 4:4–5 (NLT)

May you grow to love and accept the *you* God is making you to be. May you walk in a new level of grace and gratitude that gives you peace and leaves others encouraged. May you be more apt to look forward with hope than you are to look back with regret. May your heart spill over with joy at the very thought of the story God is writing with your life. Rest in His love.

A Quiet Place

Then, because so many people were coming and going that they did not even have a chance to eat, [Jesus] said to them, "Come with me by yourselves to a quiet place and get some rest."

Mark 6:31 (NIV)

May you put a high priority on rest and replenishment. May you make a plan to get away and nourish your soul. May you do your work with great excellence. May you take on a challenge that stretches your faith and increases your dependence on God. May your work be especially satisfying and your rest be especially sweet. Life is good that way. Bless you!

Fearing God, Not Man

Fearing people is a dangerous trap, but trusting the Lord means safety.

Proverbs 29:25 (NLT)

May you be content to know that you cannot be all things to all people; you live to serve an audience of One. May you love people but keep your hope in God. May you be willing to take risks with people, but may your sole trust be in God. May the power you once gave to others rest solely on God because He defines, He saves, He provides, and He has the power to transform.

God's Powerful Love

The Lord your God is in your midst, a mighty one who will save; he will rejoice over you with gladness; he will quiet you by his love; he will exult over you with loud singing.

Zephaniah 3:17 (ESV)

May God fine-tune your spiritual ears so you hear heaven's song above the chaos and the noise. May you rest in the knowledge that God is in control and will have the last say when it's all said and done. Though the elements rage and the enemy taunts, God is the one who fights for you and He will win for you. He loves you with power and with passion. May His kingdom come and His will be done everywhere you place your feet today. Have a powerful day in Him!

Your Influence Matters

When she speaks she has something worthwhile to
say, and she always says it kindly.

Proverbs 31:26 (MESSAGE)

In the days ahead, may you die to the power of others'
opinions and instead live out of the relentless, abundant
love God has for you. As people become more cruel and
careless with their opinions, may you become more loving
and discerning with yours. May you speak with precision,
pray with power, and stand in courage. Your life and influence matter deeply in this desperate world. Lean in and learn
everything you can from the One who loves you deeply and
intends to use you greatly.

Remember His Love

Let all that I am praise the Lord; with my whole heart,
I will praise his holy name. Let all that I am praise the
Lord; may I never forget the good things he does for me.

Psalm 103:1–2 (NLT)

May you determine to be done with captivity! No
more rehearsing your failures or rehashing your
critics' accusations. It's time to remember God's love, His
faithfulness, and His heart of affection for you. It's time to put
all of your hope in the finished work of Jesus Christ. May you
put a flag in the ground this day and declare, "My hope is built
on nothing less than Jesus' blood and righteousness!" Rest
in God's grace. Rely on His love. And rehearse His promises,
because they're true for you.

You're Made New

And we all, who with unveiled faces contemplate the Lord's glory, are being transformed into his image with ever-increasing glory, which comes from the Lord, who is the Spirit.

2 Corinthians 3:18 (NIV)

May you begin to see yourself as Christ sees you. May you understand, on a whole new level, the implications of your royal identity in Him. In Christ you are a new creation! Old things—your sins, your mistakes, your missteps—have passed away, and He's made you new, through and through. May your unveiled face reflect His glory in ever-increasing measures as you walk intimately with Him. You are His beloved treasure. Believe it today!

Remember What's True

Finally, my brethren, be strong in the Lord and in the power of His might.

Ephesians 6:10 (NKJV)

May God fill you with grace and power this very hour! May His love compel you to look up and remember what's true. May crystal-clear clarity replace confusion and chaos. And today, may you march onward with this truth alive in your soul: God is with you, He goes before you, and He has your back. You are *more* than your circumstances. You are someone God loves and empowers to live valiantly. Blessings on your day today.

Entrust Your Cares

Truly my soul silently waits for God; from Him comes my salvation.

Psalm 62:1 (NKJV)

May you open your hands and entrust your cares to God. Right this minute. Know this: Jesus knows your name, has your address, and loves who you are. He will get you where you need to go. He will reach out to the ones you love. He will validate and vindicate you at the proper time. May you see and believe that you're safest when you're at His feet, trusting Him to do what you cannot do for yourself. May your soul find rest in Him today.

You Will Overcome

I listen carefully to what God the Lord is saying, for he speaks peace to his faithful people. But let them not return to their foolish ways.

Psalm 85:8 (NLT)

May you step back from the things that frustrate you and consider what God might be saying to you here. Is He asking you to lay down your arms and entrust your soul to Him? Or is He asking you to raise your shield and stand in faith? Either way, you're not at the mercy of your circumstances. You have His mercy and He'll keep you steady and sturdy in your faith. Don't take the bait of offense. Look up and do what Jesus tells you to do. You will overcome!

Live Generously

You will be enriched in every way so that you can be generous on every occasion, and through us your generosity will result in thanksgiving to God.

2 Corinthians 9:11 (NIV)

May you suddenly know and believe that you are deeply loved, abundantly cared for, and profoundly called. May you discern the heavenly resources you've yet to lay hold of. May you begin to care more and more about the needs of others. May you give generously as one who has an endless supply to draw from. You are loved, called, equipped, and provided for. Live boldly and gladly today. The Savior has you in His hand and in His heart.

About the Author

Susie Larson is a radio host, author, and national speaker. She hosts her own daily live talk show, *Live the Promise with Susie Larson*, which airs across the upper Midwest and in several other locations around the country. Active in local ministry, she is the author of 12 books, including *Your Beautiful Purpose* and *Blessings for the Morning*. Susie and her husband, Kevin, have three adult sons and three amazing daughters-in-law and live near Minneapolis, Minnesota. For more information, visit www.susielarson.com.

MORE BLESSINGS
FROM SUSIE

Visit susielarson.com for a full list of her books.

   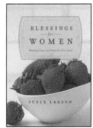

Begin and end each day with a reminder that God loves you with a passionate, everlasting love. Give Jesus your worries and obligations, and let Him nourish your heart, comfort your soul, and show you wisdom from His Word. Each blessing and related Scripture takes only moments to read, but is packed with a hope-filled, biblical perspective that will bring you joy and peace.

INSPIRATION
FROM SUSIE

Visit susielarson.com for a full list of her books.

Through personal stories and biblical insights, Susie Larson shares the secrets to effective prayer in this warm and wise book. You'll be amazed at what your prayers can do when you combine reverence, expectation, and a tenacious hold on God's promises. Discover how to pray specifically and persistently with faith and joy!

Your Powerful Prayers

It's so easy to give away our time to things un-appointed by God. In this practical and liberating book, Susie invites you to say no to overcommitment and yes to the life of joy, passion, and significance God has for you.

Your Sacred Yes

BETHANYHOUSE